Super juices

igloobooks

igloobooks

Published in 2016
by Igloo Books Ltd
Cottage Farm
Sywell
NN6 0BJ
www.igloobooks.com

Cover designed by Charles Wood-Penn
Designed by Charles Wood-Penn
Edited by Natalie Baker

Cover image © iStock / Getty

LEO002 0316
2 4 6 8 10 9 7 5 3 1
ISBN: 978-1-78557-340-8

Printed and manufactured in China

Contents

Introduction

Healthy, organic plant-based foods seem to be the latest trend at the moment. There are hundreds of raw food and juice businesses on the market – it's hard to keep up! But what are the benefits to eating this way and are we really healthier in the long run? Studies have shown that eating organic, unprocessed food is better for us and the environment. Foods that have a long shelf life are often packed with nasty chemicals and preservatives, which can have a serious impact on our health. There is a lot of bad press around refined sugars at the moment, and further evidence supports their link to chronic diseases such as obesity and diabetes. So how can we ensure that the food we eat is nutritious and delicious?

Why juice?

Juicing is a quick and easy way to get all the essential vitamins required to function properly. All you need to get started is a good juicer and a variety of fresh fruits and vegetables for your creations. Home-made juice contains natural sugars as well as plenty of fibre to improve digestive health. Juices and smoothies can be built for purpose if you use the right combination of ingredients. This book includes recipes that energize, fuel, detox and protect our bodies.

Fresh juice contains vitamins, minerals, essential fatty acids, carbohydrates, protein and much more. You will discover the benefits of juicing over time, including weight-loss, clear skin, increased energy levels and a strengthened immune system. It's so easy to incorporate juicing into your lifestyle, whether it's a morning smoothie or midday pick-me-up. Join the juice revolution today!

About Juicing

Juicing benefits

Drinking fresh fruit and vegetable juices is a simple, healthy way to ensure you are getting the vitamins and minerals you need for a balanced diet. Liquefying fruits and vegetables in a masticating or centrifugal home juicer makes consuming large amounts of produce easy, delicious and gentle on the digestive system.

The benefits of juicing are endless: energizing naturally, replacing meals with wholesome, easy-to-digest ingredients, detoxifying your system and enhancing your immunity, among many others. In addition, drinking healthy juices can help you form healthy-eating habits easily. Some regular juicers claim that juicing even helps with weight loss.

The recipes

This book is organized into four main chapters for different needs throughout the day: light, energizing juices to start your morning and rev up your metabolism; denser, fibrous juices to fuel you or substitute a light meal; cleansing juices with diuretic properties to detoxify your body; and antioxidant, antibacterial and anti-inflammatory rich drinks to protect your body from illness and combat dehydration.

Whether you have never juiced before or like to do juice cleanses regularly, turn the page to discover all the tips, tricks and knowledge you will need.

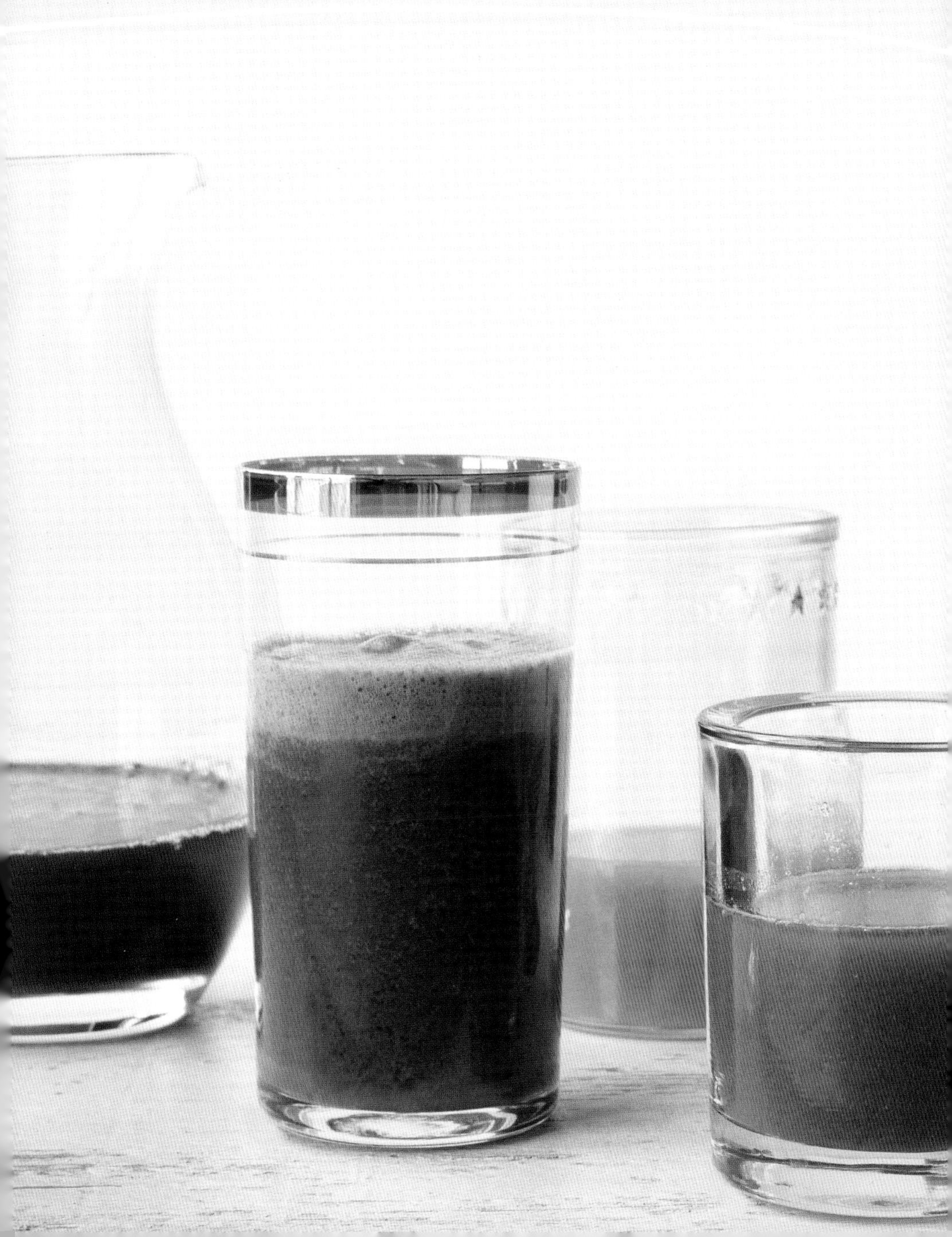

Why juice?

There is so much to love about juicing – it's healthy, hydrating and energizing, and the flavour combinations are endless. It's the proverbial golden ticket to fuelling your body with mouth-watering, tasty, healthy nutrients. Once you have experienced the benefits in these vitamin-loaded juices, you'll find them hard to resist!

It can be all too easy to spend lots of money on bottled juices, which can sometimes contain fillers, like high-moisture lettuce or excess water, and making juices at home can be much cheaper. Electric juicers may seem pricey at first; remember, you're not just investing in the machine, but also a healthy lifestyle.

Juice on the go

For many people, juicing has become part of their lifestyle. For some, mornings might begin with juicing for the family: anything from simple, fresh orange juice to kale and beetroot concoctions. For others, juicing may be part of the daily schedule: enjoyed in the morning, after a work out, or before a client meeting.

However it works best for you, juicing can help to keep you hydrated and energized throughout the day. However, juicing isn't just a solution for energy – it's a simple way to reboot your body and boost your immune system while on the run.

Juice at home

Spending a small amount at a local market goes a long way towards providing a week's worth of juices. In fact, juicing at home, as opposed to buying the bottled stuff, gets you double for your money: you not only get a delicious juice, but you also get the dehydrated fibre, or pulp, that's left behind. There are lots of great uses for this pulp: you can use vegetable fibre for the base of stocks or in muffins; nut fibre can be sprinkled over salads or used in cookies; fruit and vegetable fibre added to pet food... the ideas are endless!

How to Juice

Why?

There are endless reasons to juice: to improve health, increase energy, lose weight, prevent diseases and more. While these results aren't guaranteed, incorporating juices into your everyday life is a positive step for your well-being.

Drinking just one juice in the morning supplies more nutrients than some people consume in a whole day. In addition, juicing provides a simplified way of preparing and consuming all your favourite produce. It is a healthy, refreshing and fast way to fulfil your body's dietary needs.

When?

Deciding when to juice is up to you. Since juicing is a great way to deliver a nutrient boost, incorporating a juice into your breakfast plan is a smart start and can boost your energy without the aid of caffeine.

If you want a quick, easy and healthy meal on-the-go, there are lots of juices that are bolstered with healthy fats and fibre to keep you satisfied. If you are preparing for a mentally or physically challenging activity, like travel, an important exam or a sports competition, there are juices to help build your immune system. If you have overindulged in food or alcohol, there are juices to help flush toxins out of your system. Over time, you will grow to enjoy these juices so much, you will drink them just because you feel like it!

How?

Juicing requires a certain level of commitment, but the long-term payoff for your health is well worth it. First, you will need to invest in a juicer. Next, in order to get the most out of your juicer, it is helpful to maintain a fresh supply of fruits and vegetables. Having an abundance and variety of produce on hand means you can fulfil any craving or health need in seconds. If you have a busy schedule, you may find juicing easier and even more enjoyable when you have a whole range of juices within arm's reach.

Most juices will stay fresh for up to 3 days in the refrigerator, or for longer in the freezer, so you can plan ahead if you have a busy schedule. (Frozen juices need a few hours in the refrigerator to thaw.) Finally, start experimenting! By mixing and matching ingredients, you will soon learn what tastes and feels good to you.

About Cleansing

A juice cleanse generally refers to a meal plan where whole foods are replaced by nutrient-dense juices up to five times a day. Such cleanses are touted as ways to give the digestive system a break, recharge your body with an influx of vitamins and minerals and sometimes lose weight. If you are thinking about cleansing, it is important to first consult your doctor or a nutritionist and map out a plan that is best suited to your health needs and personal goals.

Juice cleansing is not for everyone, especially young children and pregnant women, and there is no guarantee of improved health or weight-loss results. If you are looking to begin a low-risk cleanse, start by replacing one meal or snack a day with a juice. Make sure to include a variety of soft and hard vegetables and fruit to ensure you are getting a balanced meal in place of your solid one.

Choosing a Juicer

Buying a juicer can be confusing. There are many different models on the market, each touting different features and benefits. This guide differentiates between the two most popular juicer models: a slow-masticating juicer and a centrifugal juicer. Below, you can read about the differences between these types of juicers and the pros and cons of each, to help you decide which model is suited to your juicing needs.

Slow-masticating juicer

A two-stage, low-speed system first crushes the food, then presses it to ensure a high juice yield without aerating the juice.

Features and benefits:

The juicing process takes a few seconds longer than with a centrifugal juicer.

The process produces less heat than in a centrifugal juicer, therefore preserves more natural enzymes.

For the highest juice yield, cut ingredients into 5 cm (2 in) pieces. Many models let you customize the amount of pulp and fibre in your juice.

The slow operating speed reduces the chance of oxidation (when juice loses some of its natural colour) and separation (froth on top and layering of juice ingredients).

The juicer delivers 35 percent more juice and maintains up to 60 percent more vitamins from certain types of fresh produce, such as herbs and leafy greens, than centrifugal models.

Some models make smoothies as well as juices.

Centrifugal juicer

A fast spinning motion shreds ingredients into a pulp, then extracts the juice from the pulp with centrifugal force.

Features and benefits:

Juice is extracted almost instantly, which is helpful for a busy schedule.

Models with a wide feeding tube mean many ingredients do not need to be pre-cut.

Some models have two speeds: low for softer ingredients, high for firmer ingredients.

The high operating speed means some oxidation (when juice loses some of its natural colour) and separation (froth on top and layering of juice ingredients) can occur.

These models extract the most juice from soft, high-moisture ingredients and extract less juice from fibrous and leafy ingredients.

Centrifugal models are generally more affordable than slow-masticating models.

Getting to know the Machine

Once you have decided which juicer works best for you, spend some time learning about its uses and features. A great way to do that is to take it apart. Understanding your juicer's design also helps to prevent future problems. Juicers are comprised of multiple pieces that work in a system to extract liquid from produce and separate the pulp. Since each juicer is built differently, consult your user's manual for the correct way to work with it.

The three universal components of any juicer are the food chute, the juice spout and the pulp spout. Before you start, prep your ingredients (trim, wash and cut, if necessary) and set them on the counter near the juicer. Have ready the vessels for collecting the juice and pulp as directed for your juicer. If you have a model with an open-and-close mechanism on the juice spout, make sure it is open before operating the machine for juice.

To begin the juicing cycle, drop the prepped produce down the food chute, alternating fibrous and juicy ingredients. Some models are equipped with a pusher to help ease the fruit and vegetables into the machine. Next, wait for the extracted juice to emerge from the juice spout and, for juicer models with an external pulp collector, the extracted pulp to be pushed out of the opposite end. Finally, clean the machine according to the manufacturer's instructions as soon as possible.

The best way to get to know your juicer and get the most out of your investment is to use it a lot. Use the recipes in these pages as inspiration, then experiment with different flavours, colours and textures. Test the settings (such as fine or coarse strainers for slow-masticating juicers or machine speeds for centrifugal juicers) to determine if you prefer your juices on the finer or the pulpier side. Experiment with different parts of the fruit or vegetable, as long as they are considered edible.

A good way to discover juice combinations you really enjoy is to make a few different glasses of single ingredient juices and then experiment by combining the juices in small portions. This allows you to discover new favourite flavours without wasting too much.

Caring for your juicer

Make the most of your equipment and fresh fruits and vegetables by keeping your juicer in top shape. An improperly functioning juicer may waste raw ingredients and will not produce the maximum amount of juice possible. If you are making multiple servings of juice, run a cup or two of water through the machine after each batch.

Be careful not to overload your juicer. For best results, consult the user's manual for your juicer to discover the right way to work with ingredients in your machine.

How to Prep Ingredients

Prepping juice ingredients usually involves simply washing the produce and cutting it to fit the food chute of your machine. Here are some additional tips for popular fruits and vegetables.

Wash whole ingredients to rid them of dirt or grit. Use a produce brush to remove stubborn, caked-on dirt.

Pare away tough skins: anything with an inedible or bitter peel, such as those on avocados and citrus, should be removed. Any peel you choose to keep intact should be thoroughly scrubbed and washed.

Remove any inedible pits. This is especially important for stone fruits, such as cherries and peaches. Small, soft seeds, like those in apples, pears and citrus, can be juiced. Papaya seeds can be juiced for extra nutrients.

Place leafy greens and herbs in a colander and plunge them into a cold-water bath. Swirl them around to remove dirt. Drain and repeat if necessary for extra-dirty greens.

For added nutrients, keep the leafy tops of vegetables and fruits intact. This includes strawberry stems, beetroot leaves, carrot tops, fennel fronds and celery leaves.

Nuts should be soaked in water for a minimum of 5 hours, but preferably 8 hours, before being juiced into milk.

The way you prep ingredients for juicing can affect the taste of the finished juice. For example, juicing citrus with and without its peel has a very different result. Some recipes call for a 'knob of ginger', which refers to a 2.5 cm (1 in) piece of fresh ginger. Peeling is optional.

Some recipes call for fresh turmeric, which resembles a small piece of ginger. It can be found at farmers' markets and health food stores. Peeling is optional.

Some ingredients, such as coconut water, coconut oil, chia seeds and others are simply stirred into the finished juice to add volume or nutrients to the juice.

About raw honey

Because raw honey is unpasteurized, it is loaded in live enzymes and antimicrobial compounds known to have antibacterial properties. You can find raw honey in many supermarkets in the baking or health food aisles. Pregnant women, young children and some people with food allergies or immune disorders should not consume raw honey. Pasteurized honey can easily replace raw honey in all these recipes.

Tips and Tricks for Juicing

One of the joys of juicing is the endless flavour options. No matter what the combination is, if your juice is made from fresh fruit or vegetables, you are doing your body a big, nutritious favour. Here are some good tips to keep in mind while experimenting.

Combine hues

The more diverse the colours that go into the juice, the more nutritious, and hopefully delicious, it will be – even if the end result is a little brownish in colour.

Colour matters

Studies show that humans are more satisfied by visually appealing food. If your juice is an off-colour, consider adding an ingredient with a strong hue, such as red beetroot, orange carrots or leafy greens. The addition of lemon juice helps retain the colour.

Think of it as a meal

Not sure what to combine to get a taste you like? Juice items that you would want to eat together in their whole form. Think of your favourite ingredients to put in a salad or eat as a snack and let that be the inspiration for your juice.

Clean out the fridge

Use juicing not only as an opportunity to clean out the vegetable bin and fruit bowl, but also to encourage you to keep them regularly stocked.

Mix textures

Combining soft, juicy produce (such as pears, cucumbers and citrus) with fibrous, firm produce (such as kale, root vegetables and nuts) makes a well-balanced juice. Because fibrous ingredients produce less liquid, it is important to combine them with moisture-rich ingredients.

Taste as you go

You can make your mixed juices by alternating ingredients in the machine, or you can collect each juiced item individually and combine the juices afterwards. If you are using the former technique, taste after each addition until you are happy.

Freezing juice

Most juices will last for a few days in the freezer. When you are ready to consume a frozen juice, thaw it for several hours in the refrigerator until it returns to a liquid state.

Storing fresh juice

For the freshest juice and highest level of nutrients, aim to drink juices within 24 hours. They can be refrigerated in airtight containers or bottles for up to 72 hours. If you are using the dehydrated fibre, or pulp, it should be used within 24 hours for best texture and flavour. Otherwise pulp can be frozen and reserved.

Juices That Energize

Energizing juices, packed with vibrant fruits and light vegetables, are a great way to start your day or supply a midday pick-me-up. Instead of reaching for the usual morning coffee, wake up your taste buds with a metabolism-boosting, energizing juice.

These juices are as clean, pure and simple as they get. Because they are extracted from ingredients with a high water density and low fibre content, they are easy for your digestive system to handle in the morning.

These are the lightest juices featured in this book, so they are best enjoyed followed by a breakfast shake, healthy solid foods, or a denser mid-afternoon juice.

Tangerine, Cherry and Apple

Makes: about 500 ml / 16 fl. oz / 2 cups

Ingredients

375 g / 12 oz / 2 cups pitted fresh sweet cherries or thawed, frozen cherries

3 tangerines

1 green apple

Method

1. Stem the cherries, if necessary. Peel the tangerines and cut the apple to fit the juicer.

2. Place the cherries, tangerines and apple into the feeder of the juice extractor, then run the machine. Enjoy as soon as possible.

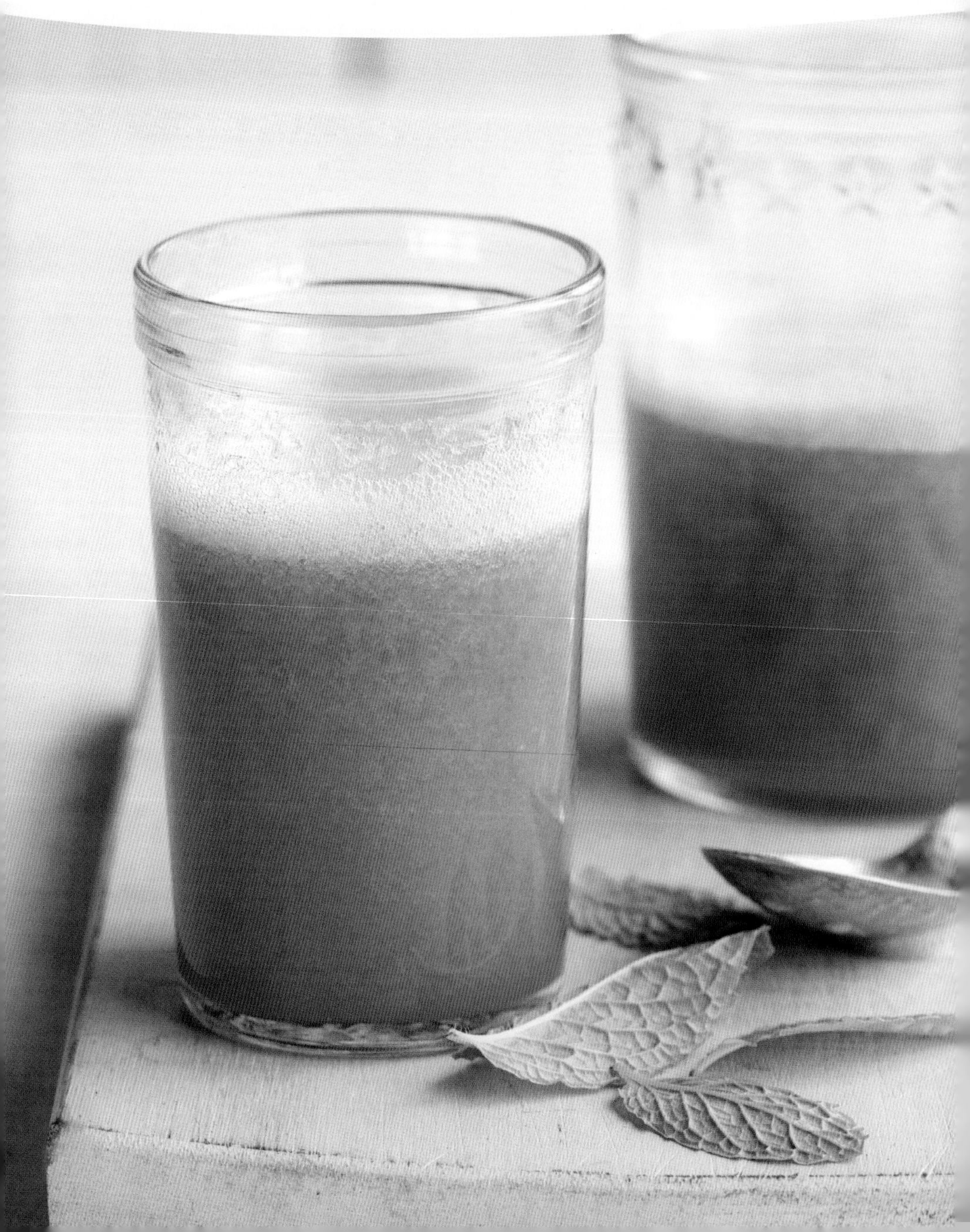

Minty Pick-Me-Up

Makes: about 625 ml / 20 fl. oz / 2 ½ cups

Ingredients

1 large pineapple

1 pear

30 fresh mint leaves

125 g / 4 oz / 1 cup strawberries

Method

1. Peel the pineapple. Cut the pineapple and pear to fit the juicer.

2. Place the pineapple, pear, mint and strawberries into the feeder of the juice extractor, then run the machine.

3. Enjoy as soon as possible.

Beetroot, Apple and Ginger

Makes: about 500 ml / 16 fl. oz / 2 cups

Ingredients

3 yellow beetroot

1 green apple

knob of ginger

Method

1. Cut the beetroot and apple to fit the juicer.

2. Place the beetroot, ginger and apple into the feeder of a juice extractor, then run the machine.

3. Enjoy as soon as possible.

Orange, Carrot and Melon

Makes: about 500 ml / 16 fl. oz / 2 cups

Ingredients

½ cantaloupe

2 oranges

8 carrots

Method

1. Peel and seed the cantaloupe.

2. Peel the oranges, then cut the cantaloupe and oranges to fit the juicer.

3. Place the cantaloupe, oranges and carrots into the feeder of the juice extractor, then run the machine.

4. Enjoy as soon as possible.

Grape Power Juice

Makes: about 500 ml / 16 fl. oz / 2 cups

Ingredients

2 bunches grapes

chia seeds

Method

1. Remove the grapes from the vine.

2. Place the grapes into the feeder of the juice extractor, then run the machine.

3. Pour the juice into a glass, stir in chia seeds to taste (start with about 1 tbsp).

4. Enjoy as soon as possible.

Revitalizing Elixir

Makes: about 500 ml / 16 fl. oz / 2 cups

Ingredients

500 g / 15 oz / 3 cups watermelon pieces

1 lime

1 cucumber

knob of ginger

Method

1. Peel the watermelon and lime.

2. Cut the watermelon, lime and cucumber to fit the juicer.

3. Place the watermelon, lime, ginger and cucumber into the feeder of the juice extractor, then run the machine.

4. Enjoy as soon as possible.

Mango, Apple and Pineapple

Makes: about 500 ml / 16 fl. oz / 2 cups

Ingredients

1 mango

1 pineapple

1 green apple

Method

1. Peel and pit the mango.

2. Peel the pineapple.

3. Cut the pineapple and apple to fit the juicer.

4. Place the mango, pineapple and apple into the feeder of a juice extractor, then run the machine.

5. Enjoy as soon as possible.

Sunshiny Day

Makes: about 500 ml / 16 fl. oz / 2 cups

Ingredients

3 oranges
¼ cantaloupe
2 green apples
10 fresh mint leaves

Method

1. Peel the oranges. Peel and de-seed the cantaloupe.
2. Cut the oranges, cantaloupe and apples to fit the juicer.
3. Place the cantaloupe, apples, oranges and mint into the feeder of a juice extractor, then run the machine.
4. Enjoy as soon as possible.

Pineapple, Banana and Strawberry

Makes: about 500 ml / 16 fl. oz / 2 cups

Ingredients

1 banana

½ pineapple

250 g / 8 oz / 1 cup strawberries

Method

1. Peel the banana.

2. Peel the pineapple and cut it to fit the juicer.

3. Place the banana, pineapple and strawberries into the feeder of the juice extractor, then run the machine.

4. Enjoy as soon as possible.

Green Day

Makes: about 500 ml / 16 fl. oz / 2 cups

Ingredients

3 kiwis

3 green apples

1 cucumber

10 fresh mint leaves

Method

1. Peel the kiwis.

2. Cut the kiwis, apples and cucumber to fit the juicer.

3. Place the kiwis, apples, mint and cucumber into the feeder of the juice extractor, then run the machine.

4. Enjoy as soon as possible.

Juices That Fuel

Inspired by salads and snacks, these dense juices are filled with a healthy variety of produce to fuel you through the day. Fibrous greens, such as kale and chard, keep you full and help control hunger swings. They're loaded with antioxidants, potassium and calcium – the darker green leaves pack more nutrients.

Just as greens serve as the base for most salads, so too do they act as the foundation for these thick juices. Continuing with the salad theme, some other ingredients have been included: sweet potatoes for stabilizing blood sugar, avocados and coconut oil for heart-healthy monounsaturated fats, and spices for a flavour kick and multitude of health benefits.

Cranberry and Banana

Makes: about 500 ml / 16 fl. oz / 2 cups

Ingredients

2 bananas

1 papaya

¼ pineapple

125 g / 4 oz / 1 cup cranberries

Method

1. Peel the bananas, papaya and pineapple.

2. Cut the papaya and pineapple to fit the juicer.

3. Place the banana, papaya, pineapple and cranberries into the feeder of a juice extractor, then run the machine.

4. Enjoy as soon as possible.

Sweet Greens

Makes: about 500 ml / 16 fl. oz / 2 cups

Ingredients

3 apples

2 beetroot

8 kale leaves

knob of ginger

Method

1. Cut the apples and beetroot to fit the juicer.

2. Place the beetroot, kale, ginger and apples into the feeder of a juice extractor, then run the machine.

3. Enjoy as soon as possible.

Sweet Carrot Milk

Makes: about 500 ml / 16 fl. oz / 2 cups

Ingredients

250 ml / 8 fl. oz / 1 cup hazelnut
(cobnut) milk (see page 72)

2 sweet potatoes

4 carrots

Method

1. Make the hazelnut milk as directed. Cut the sweet potatoes to fit the juicer.

2. Place the sweet potatoes and carrots into the feeder of a juice extractor, then run the machine.

3. Pour the juice into a glass, stir in the hazelnut milk and enjoy as soon as possible.

Tropical Boost

Makes: about 500 ml / 16 fl. oz / 2 cups

Ingredients

250 ml / 8 fl. oz / 1 cup Brazil nut milk
(see page 72)

2 mangoes

¼ pineapple

Method

1. Make the Brazil nut milk as directed.
   Peel and pit the mangoes.

2. Peel the pineapple and cut to fit the juicer.

3. Place the mango and pineapple into
   the feeder of a juice extractor, then run
   the machine.

4. Pour the juice into a glass, mix in the Brazil
   nut milk and enjoy as soon as possible.

Mexican Chocolate Milk

Makes: about 500 ml / 16 fl. oz / 2 cups

Ingredients

500 ml / 16 fl. oz / 2 cups hazelnut milk
(see page 72)

2 tbsp cacao powder

pinch of cayenne pepper

3 tbsp raw honey

pinch of ground cinnamon

Method

1. Make the hazelnut milk as directed.

2. Mix together the hazelnut milk, cacao powder, cayenne, honey and cinnamon.

3. Pour into a glass and enjoy as soon as possible.

Super Salad

Makes: about 500 ml / 16 fl. oz / 2 cups

Ingredients

2 cucumbers

1 apple

6 kale leaves

60 g / 2 oz / 2 cups spinach

3 stalks celery

3 carrots

Method

1. Cut the cucumbers and apple to fit the juicer.

2. Place the kale, spinach, cucumbers, celery, carrots and apple into the feeder of a juice extractor, then run the machine.

3. Enjoy as soon as possible.

Green Dream

Makes: about 500 ml / 16 fl. oz / 2 cups

Ingredients

2 kiwis

1 lemon

1 green apple

1 cucumber

½ bunch kale

½ head romaine lettuce

Method

1. Peel the kiwis and lemon.

2. Cut the kiwis, lemon, apple and cucumber to fit the juicer.

3. Place the kiwi, kale, lemon, romaine, cucumber and apple into the feeder of a juice extractor, then run the machine.

4. Enjoy as soon as possible.

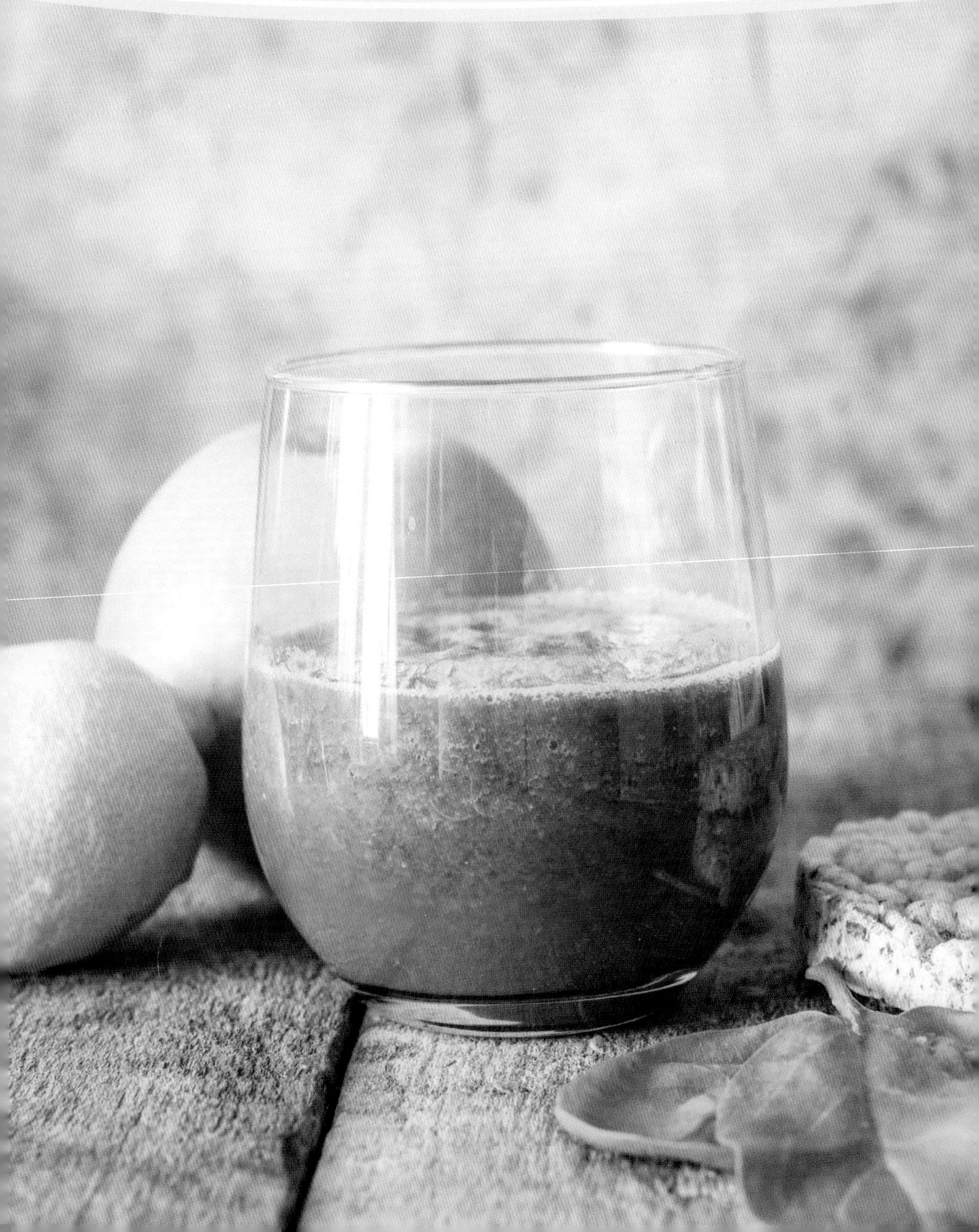

Apple and Spinach Harmony

Makes: about 500 ml / 16 fl. oz / 2 cups

Ingredients

1 lemon

2 ½ green apples

1 pear

45 g / 1 ½ oz / 1 ½ cups spinach

1 celery stalk

Method

1. Peel the lemon and cut the lemon, apples and pear to fit the juicer.

2. Place the lemon, apples, pear, spinach and celery into the feeder of a juice extractor, then run the machine.

3. Enjoy as soon as possible.

Basic Nut Milk

Makes: about 250 ml / 8 fl. oz / 1 cup

Ingredients

75 g / 2 ½ oz / ½ cup nuts, such as
almonds, Brazil nuts, cashews or
hazelnuts (cobnuts)

250 ml / 8 fl. oz / 1 cup filtered water,
plus more for soaking

½ tbsp maple syrup (optional)

pinch of salt (optional)

Method

1. Soak the nuts in a bowl of water for at least
5 hours and up to 24 hours.

2. Drain the nuts, then place the nuts and the
filtered water into the feeder of a juice
extractor and run the machine.

3. Pour the milk into a glass, stir in the maple
syrup and salt, if using, and enjoy as soon
as possible.

Triple Greens

Makes: about 500 ml / 16 fl. oz / 2 cups

Ingredients

½ head romaine lettuce

½ bunch kale or collard greens

30 g / 1 oz / 1 cup spinach

½ bunch fresh flat-leaf parsley

2 celery stalks

1 tbsp coconut oil

Method

1. Place the romaine, kale or collards, spinach, parsley and celery into the feeder of a juice extractor, then run the machine.

2. Pour the juice into a glass, stir in the coconut oil and enjoy as soon as possible.

Juices That Detoxify

Maybe you went just a little overboard, indulging in a few too many rich foods and alcoholic drinks? Consuming a bit too much happens to the best of us, especially during holidays and celebratory events. Luckily, juices can be a remedy.

Detoxifying juices are made with ingredients that boost liver and digestive functions. These help flush out toxins as well as replenish your system with vitamin B, which is depleted while consuming alcohol or processed foods.

Nutrient-dense, electrolyte-packed drinks replace toxins with an abundant variety of vitamins and minerals to keep your system strong while it cleanses. Citrus, spices, chillies and colourful vegetables keep the combinations delicious and varied.

Sweet Escape

Makes: about 500 ml / 16 fl. oz / 2 cups

Ingredients

4 mandarin oranges

1 lime

6 guavas

125 g / 4 oz / 1 cup strawberries

Method

1. Peel the oranges and lime.

2. Cut the oranges, lime and guavas to fit the juicer.

3. Place the oranges, lime, guavas and strawberries into the feeder of a juice extractor, then run the machine.

4. Enjoy as soon as possible.

Deep Red Potion

Makes: about 500 ml / 16 fl. oz / 2 cups

Ingredients

1 lime

3 tomatoes

2 cucumbers

1 beetroot

Method

1. Peel the lime.

2. Cut the lime, tomatoes, cucumbers and beetroot to fit the juicer.

3. Place the lime, tomatoes, cucumbers and beetroot into the feeder of a juice extractor, then run the machine.

4. Enjoy as soon as possible.

Anti-inflammatory Tonic

Makes: about 500 ml / 16 fl. oz / 2 cups

Ingredients

1 cantaloupe, de-seeded

1 lime

1 small fresh turmeric root

½ jalapeño

8 basil leaves

250 ml / 8 fl. oz / 1 cup coconut water

Method

1. Peel and de-seed the cantaloupe.

2. Peel the lime. Cut the cantaloupe and lime to fit the juicer.

3. Place the cantaloupe, turmeric, jalapeño, basil and lime into the feeder of a juice extractor, then run the machine.

4. Pour the juice into a glass, stir in the coconut water and enjoy as soon as possible.

Ginger and Asian Pear

Makes: about 500 ml / 16 fl. oz / 2 cups

Ingredients

2 lemons

6 Asian pears

knob of ginger

Method

1. Peel the lemons and cut the lemons and pears to fit the juicer.

2. Place the pears, ginger and lemons into the feeder of a juice extractor, then run the machine.

3. Enjoy as soon as possible.

Beetroot, Apple and Coconut

Makes: about 500 ml / 16 fl. oz / 2 cups

Ingredients

4 red apples

3 red beetroot

250 ml / 8 fl. oz / 1 cup coconut water

Method

1. Cut the apples and beetroot to fit the juicer.

2. Place the apples and beetroot into the feeder of a juice extractor, then run the machine.

3. Pour the juice into a glass, stir in the coconut water and enjoy as soon as possible.

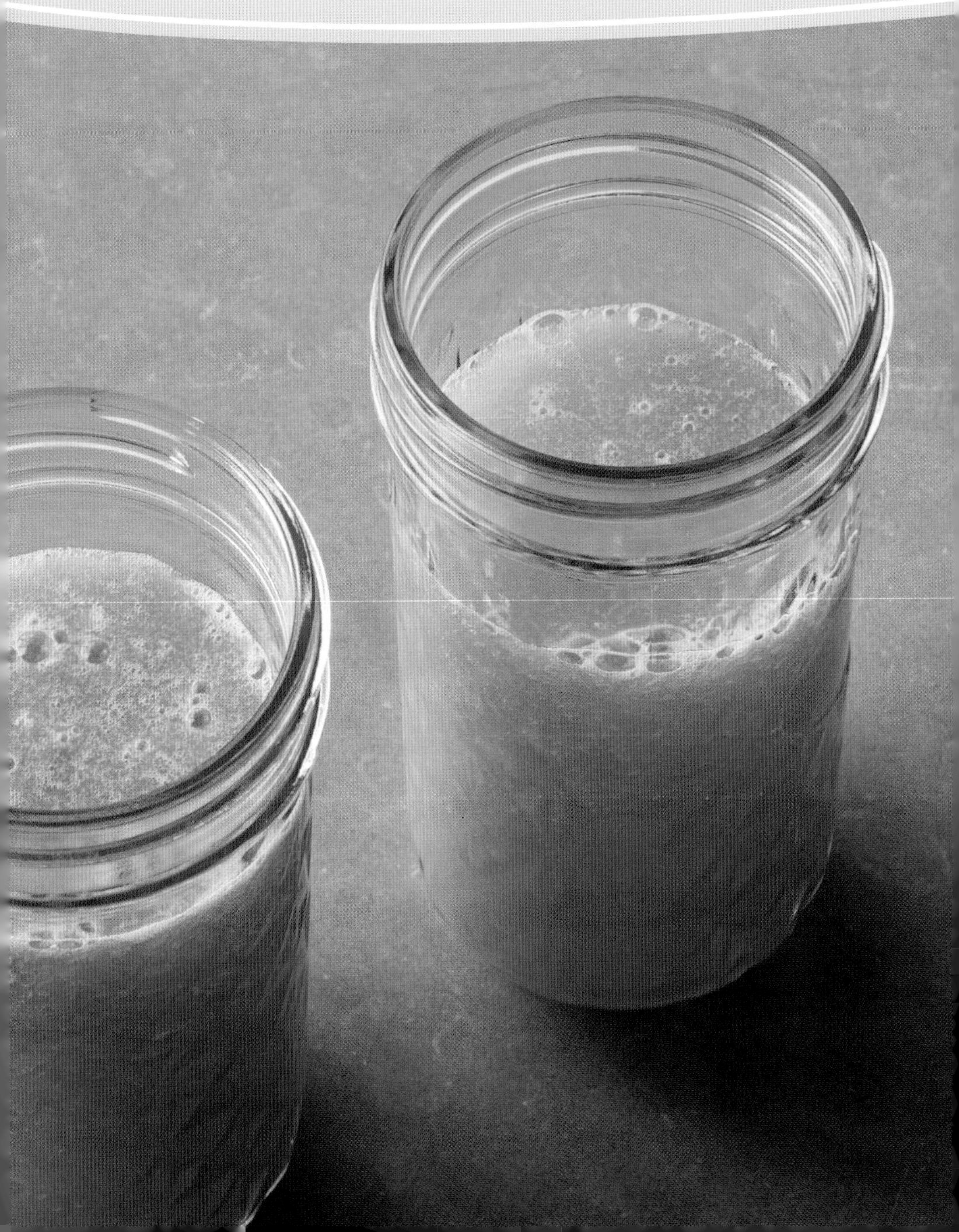

Tropical Spice

Makes: about 500 ml / 16 fl. oz / 2 cups

Ingredients

1 papaya

¼ pineapple

1 pear

1 jalapeño

Method

1. Peel the papaya and pineapple.

2. Cut the papaya, pineapple and pear to fit the juicer.

3. Place the papaya, pineapple, jalapeño and pear into the feeder of a juice extractor, then run the machine.

4. Enjoy as soon as possible.

Orange Zinger

Makes: about 500 ml / 16 fl. oz / 2 cups

Ingredients

2 ripe fuyu persimmons

knob of ginger

1 small fresh turmeric root

125 g / 4 oz / 1 cup pomegranate seeds

4 carrots

Method

1. Remove the stems from the persimmons and cut to fit the juicer.

2. Place the persimmons, ginger, turmeric, pomegranate seeds and carrots into the feeder of a juice extractor, then run the machine.

3. Enjoy as soon as possible.

Superfood Detox

Makes: about 500 ml / 16 fl. oz / 2 cups

Ingredients

1 orange

155 g / 5 oz / 1 cup watermelon pieces

1 beetroot

250 g / 8 oz / 2 cups pomegranate seeds

250 g / 8 oz / 1 pt raspberries

Method

1. Peel the orange and watermelon.

2. Cut the orange, watermelon and beetroot to fit the juicer.

3. Place the orange, watermelon, beetroot, pomegranate seeds and raspberries into the feeder of a juice extractor, then run the machine.

4. Enjoy as soon as possible.

Tropical Virgin Mary Juice

Makes: about 500 ml / 16 fl. oz / 2 cups

Ingredients

¼ pineapple

2 tomatoes

1 small piece fresh horseradish, or 1 tbsp
prepared horseradish

2 celery stalks

¼ bunch fresh parsley

½ head red leaf lettuce

Method

1. Peel the pineapple and cut the pineapple and tomatoes to fit the juicer.

2. Place the pineapple, horseradish, celery, parsley, lettuce and tomatoes into the feeder of a juice extractor, then run the machine.

3. Enjoy as soon as possible.

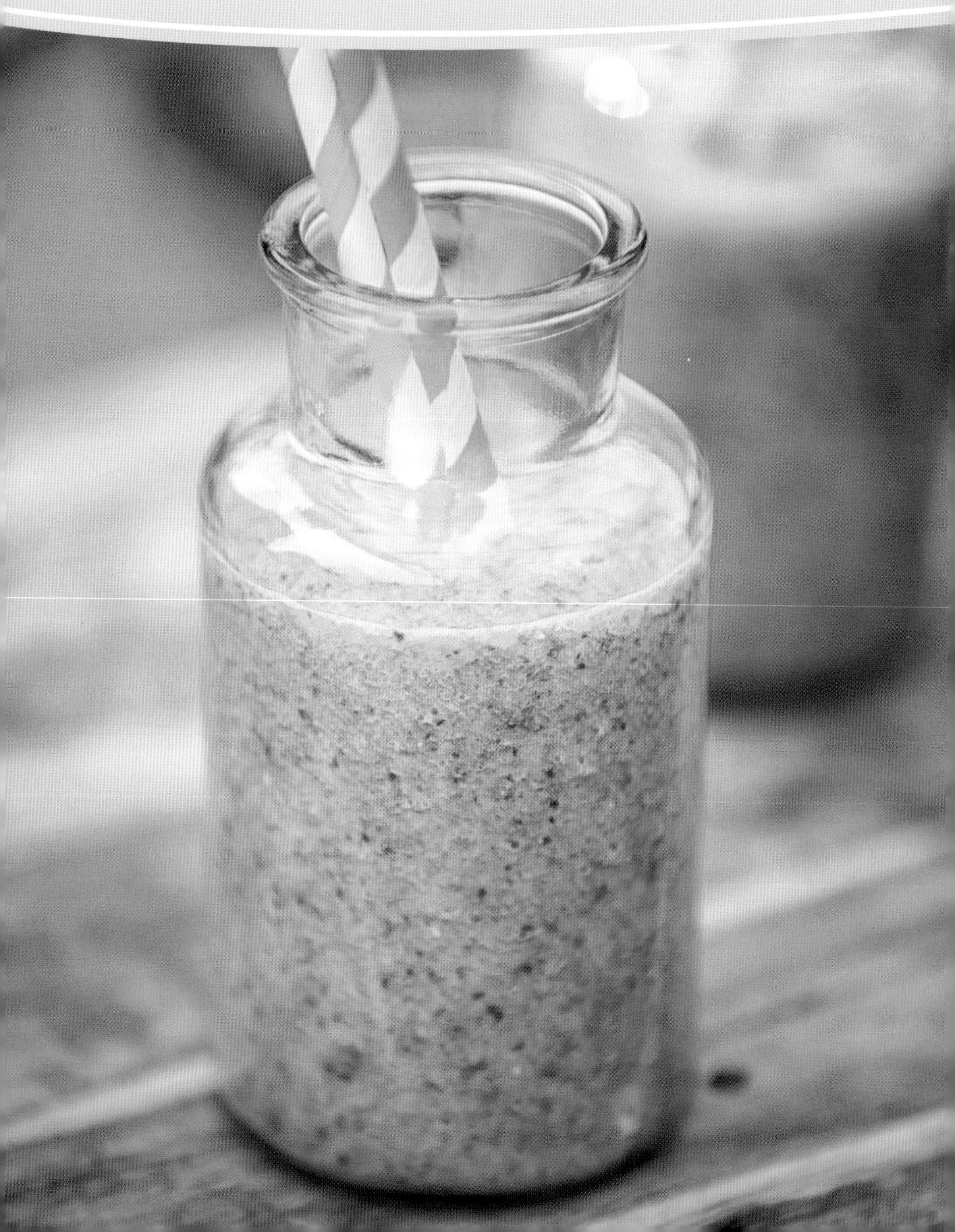

Spinach and Parsley Purifier

Makes: about 500 ml / 16 fl. oz / 2 cups

Ingredients

1 lemon

3 green apples

120 g / 4 oz / 4 cups spinach

1 bunch fresh parsley

½ jalapeño

Method

1. Peel the lemon and cut the lemon and apples to fit the juicer.

2. Place the apples, spinach, parsley, jalapeño and lemon into the feeder of a juice extractor, then run the machine.

3. Enjoy as soon as possible.

Juices That Protect

These immunity-boosting elixirs are perhaps the most vital type of juice to incorporate into a diet. Protecting our bodies means making them strong enough to fight against germs, destructive bone, organ and blood diseases and the wear-and-tear of stress and missed sleep.

These drinks make excellent daily supplements to keep your immune system strong, but are also great to drink before and after physically demanding events.

Juices with immune-boosting qualities can help safeguard you through cold and flu season, keeping your body balanced. Don't limit these drinks for just the bad times – keep them in your daily routine to aid your health all year long.

Blueberry Blast

Makes: about 500 ml / 16 fl. oz / 2 cups

Ingredients

1 grapefruit

1 lime

2 apples

250 g / 8 oz / 2 cups blueberries

2 carrots

Method

1. Peel the grapefruit and lime and cut the grapefruit, lime and apples to fit the juicer.

2. Place the grapefruit, lime, apples, blueberries and carrots into the feeder of a juice extractor, then run the machine.

3. Enjoy as soon as possible.

Potent Protector

Makes: about 500 ml / 16 fl. oz / 2 cups

Ingredients

2 pomegranates

1 grapefruit

knob of ginger

4 carrots

Method

1. Remove the seeds from the pomegranates. Peel the grapefruit and cut to fit the juicer.

2. Place the pomegranate seeds, grapefruit, ginger and carrots into the feeder of a juice extractor, then run the machine.

3. Enjoy as soon as possible.

Honeydew-Kiwi Cooler

Makes: about 500 ml / 16 fl. oz / 2 cups

Ingredients

½ honeydew melon

4 kiwis

1 lime

Method

1. Peel the melon, kiwis and lime and cut to fit the juicer.

2. Place the melon, kiwi and lime into the feeder of a juice extractor, then run the machine.

3. Enjoy as soon as possible.

Berry and Pomegranate

Makes: about 500 ml / 16 fl. oz / 2 cups

Ingredients

3 pomegranates

500 g / 16 oz / 2 pt blackberries

500 g / 16 oz / 2 pt blueberries

Method

1. De-seed the pomegranates.

2. Place the pomegranate seeds, blackberries and blueberries (or 500 g / 16 oz / 2 pt total mixed berries) into the feeder of a juice extractor, then run the machine.

3. Enjoy as soon as possible.

Carrot Sunrise

Makes: about 500 ml / 16 fl. oz / 2 cups

Ingredients

1 orange
½ lemon
¼ pineapple
2 carrots

Method

1. Peel the orange, lemon and pineapple and cut to fit the juicer.

2. Place the orange, lemon, pineapple and carrots into the feeder of a juice extractor, then run the machine.

3. Enjoy as soon as possible.

Brassica Bomb

Makes: about 500 ml / 16 fl. oz / 2 cups

Ingredients

1 lemon

2 pears

2 apples

185 g / 6 oz / 2 cups chopped cabbage

8 kale leaves

Method

1. Peel the lemon and cut the lemon, pears and apples to fit the juicer.

2. Place the lemon, pears, cabbage, kale and apples into the feeder of a juice extractor, then run the machine.

3. Enjoy as soon as possible.

Berry Supreme

Makes: about 500 ml / 16 fl. oz / 2 cups

Ingredients

125 g / 4 oz / 1 cup raspberries

125 g / 4 oz / 1 cup blueberries

125 g / 4 oz / 1 cup fresh or thawed, frozen cranberries

250 ml / 8 fl. oz / 1 cup coconut water

2 tbsp raw honey

Method

1. Place the raspberries, blueberries and cranberries into the feeder of a juice extractor, then run the machine.

2. Pour the juice into a glass, stir in the coconut water and honey.

3. Enjoy as soon as possible.

Recharger

Makes: about 500 ml / 16 fl. oz / 2 cups

Ingredients

2 oranges

2 tangerines

250 g / 8 oz / 2 cups blueberries

2 tbsp chia seeds

Method

1. Peel the oranges and tangerines and cut to fit the juicer.

2. Place the blueberries, oranges and tangerines into the feeder of a juice extractor, then run the machine.

3. Pour the juice into a glass, stir in the chia seeds and enjoy as soon as possible.

Orange Boost

Makes: about 500 ml / 16 fl. oz / 2 cups

Ingredients

1 lemon

1 orange

1 papaya

1 small fresh turmeric

knob of ginger

8 carrots

Method

1. Peel the lemon, orange and papaya and cut to fit the juicer.

2. Place the lemon, orange, papaya, turmeric, ginger and carrots into the feeder of a juice extractor, then run the machine.

3. Enjoy as soon as possible.

Spicy Ps

Makes: about 500 ml / 16 fl. oz / 2 cups

Ingredients

1 papaya
¼ pineapple
1 pear
1 jalapeño

Method

1. Peel the papaya and pineapple.

2. Cut the papaya, pineapple and pear to fit the juicer.

3. Place the papaya, pineapple, jalapeño and pear into the feeder of a juice extractor, then run the machine.

4. Enjoy as soon as possible.

Energizing Ingredients

Apples: Apples are high in quercetin, a flavonoid that slows the digestive process of carbohydrates, helping to prolong energy storage and regulate blood sugar.

Fresh mint: The strong aroma of mint activates the salivary glands, which secrete digestive enzymes, promoting healthy digestive functions.

Grapes: Red and black grapes are an excellent source of the antioxidant manganese, which can help regulate blood sugar. Naturally sweet in taste, grapes are surprisingly low on the glycemic index.

Kiwis: Kiwis are an exceptional source of vitamin C, which is a natural energy provider. With a low glycemic index, kiwis will steady your blood sugar, helping you to feel full and satisfied over time.

Mangoes: High levels of potassium can help control blood pressure and keep you feeling full for a long time. Mangoes are full of enzymes that break down protein, which helps improve digestion.

Pineapples: Pineapples are an excellent source of vitamin C, which is a natural energy provider. The high levels of vitamin B may help with digestion. They also contain compounds that help increase circulation.

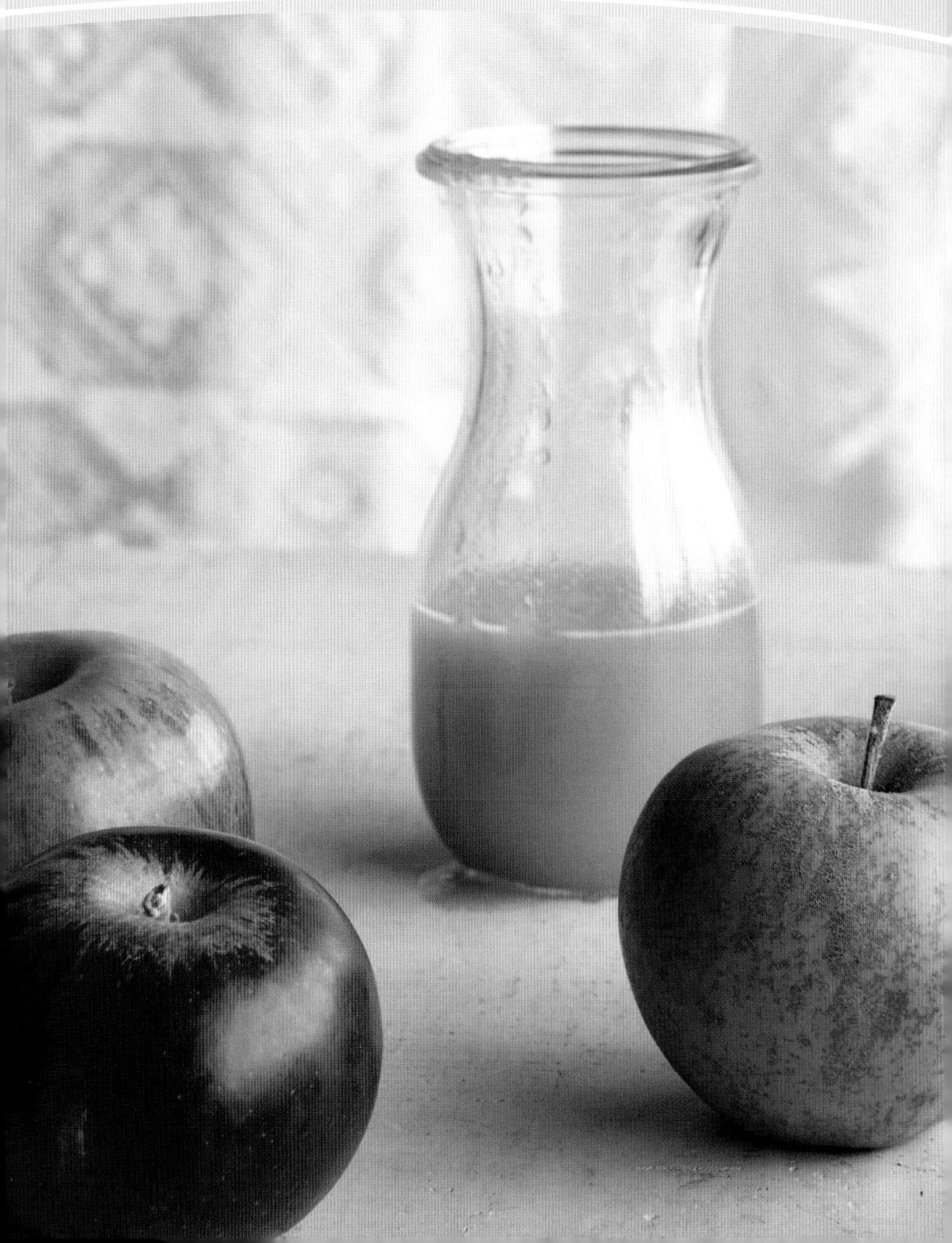

Fuelling Ingredients

Avocados: Creamy avocados are full of good-for-you monounsaturated fats, which have been shown to aid the body's absorption of antioxidants while also protecting the heart and joints. Avocados' buttery consistency lends smoothness to juices.

Chard: Chard and other leafy greens are bursting with calcium. Their crunchy stems are rich in fibre, which can help control hunger. If your juicer has a pulp control lever, choose the 'close' setting for pulpier juices with more fibre.

Kale: Kale is bursting in beta-carotene, carotenoids, vitamin A and calcium. Its high fibre content can help keep you to feel fuller for longer. If your juicer has a pulp control lever, choose the 'close' setting to get pulpier juices with more fibre. Some juice aficionados like to chew pulpy green juice to help process its beneficial fibre.

Nuts: Nuts are full of protein and healthy monounsaturated fat. Soak them in water and run them through the juicer for a naturally creamy, dairy-free milk. Brazil nuts are one of the best varieties for making creamy milk that is rich in healthy fats. Almonds, hazelnuts (cobnuts) and cashews also produce delicious, naturally sweet nut milks.

Sweet potatoes: The darker the flesh of a sweet potato, the richer it is in phytonutrients. These root vegetables are loaded with good carbohydrates that help stabilize blood sugar.

Detoxifying Ingredients

Chillies (chilies): Capsaicin, the active component that gives chillies their fiery taste, is known to help speed digestion, clear upper-body congestion, help reduce cholesterol and relieve head and joint aches. Plus, it adds a nice bite to your favourite juice.

Coconut water: Like plain H_2O, coconut water works as a diuretic to help flush toxins out of the system, while also keeping the body hydrated. Non-concentrate coconut water can help with rehydration, since it is full of electrolytes. It also adds a subtle, natural sweetness to juice blends.

Ginger: Ginger has been shown to relax and soothe the intestinal tract, while promoting the elimination of internal toxins.

Lemons and limes: Citrus is a great source of vitamin C, which can help to boost the immune system and provide natural energy. Both fruits add a refreshing zing to drinks.

Melons: Nearly 90 per cent water, watermelons and other melons are rich in nutrients and low in calories. Watermelons are high in vitamin C and contain the antioxidant lycopene. Cantaloupe and honeydew boast vitamins C, B and A, as well as potassium.

Tomatoes: Tomato juice has been known to reduce cholesterol and work as a natural antiseptic. The acidity in tomatoes helps activate the liver, which plays a key role in detoxifying.

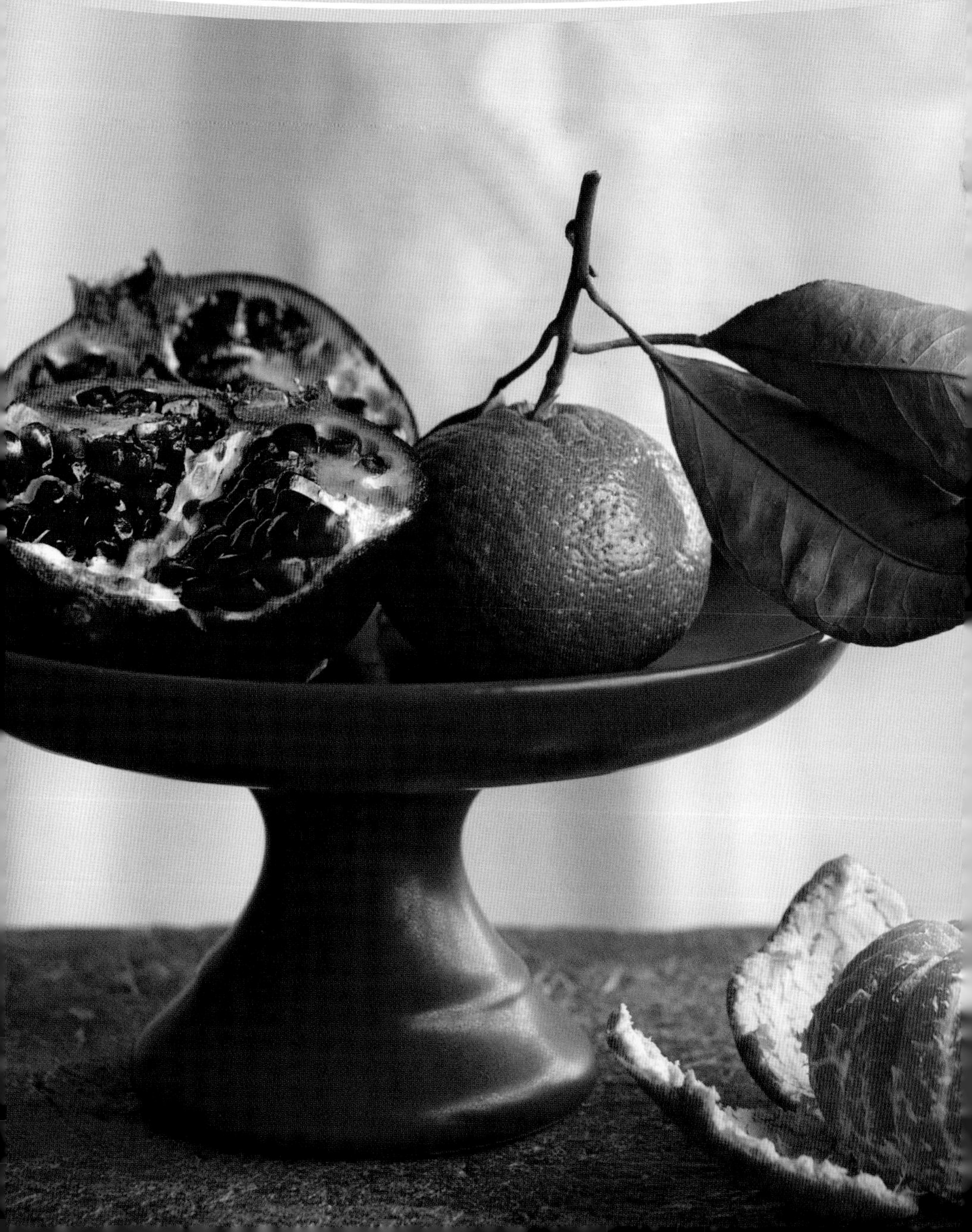

Protecting Ingredients

Blueberries: These dark-coloured fruits are a powerful source of antioxidants that have been linked to improved memory. They are also rich in flavonoids, which help contribute to heart health.

Carrots: Carrots are renowned for being good for your eyes. They are high in vitamin A, beta-carotene and good-for-you carotenoids.

Chillies (chilies): Hot chillies, such as jalapeños, serranos and Thai chillies, are high in vitamins A and C, which have been known to prevent infections and boost the immune system.

Oranges: Citrus fruits are rich in vitamin C and potassium, both of which have been shown to boost the immune system and help ward off illness.

Pomegranates: The juice of these tree fruits contains powerful antioxidant substances that protect cells from oxidation. They are also a good source of vitamin C, which is known to support the immune system.